A+ books

WORLD OF COLORS

Egypt in Colors

by Nathan Olson

Consultant: Kathleen Scanlan Scott
Director of Publications
The American Research Center in Egypt

Capstone press

Mankato, Minnesota

Brown pyramids tower over the dry desert. The ancient Egyptians built the pyramids about 4,500 years ago. They used them to bury their rulers. Today, many tourists visit the pyramids on the back of a camel.

A student makes an ancient Egyptian symbol using **orange** paint. Besides art and history, students study reading, writing, math, science, and Arabic. Most children ages 6 to 14 go to school.

Metalworkers make **golden** lanterns for Ramadan. Ramadan is a holiday that lasts for one month. Muslims fast during the day. At night, families gather together for meals. Children sing and swing their colorful lanterns.

Many Egyptians wear **white** clothing in the desert. The light color helps keep them cool. Part of the cloth can be used to protect the face from blowing sand.

Purple grapes, **yellow** lemons, and **red** tomatoes are for sale at an Egyptian food stand. Many Egyptians work on farms. Farmers sell their crops at outdoor markets.

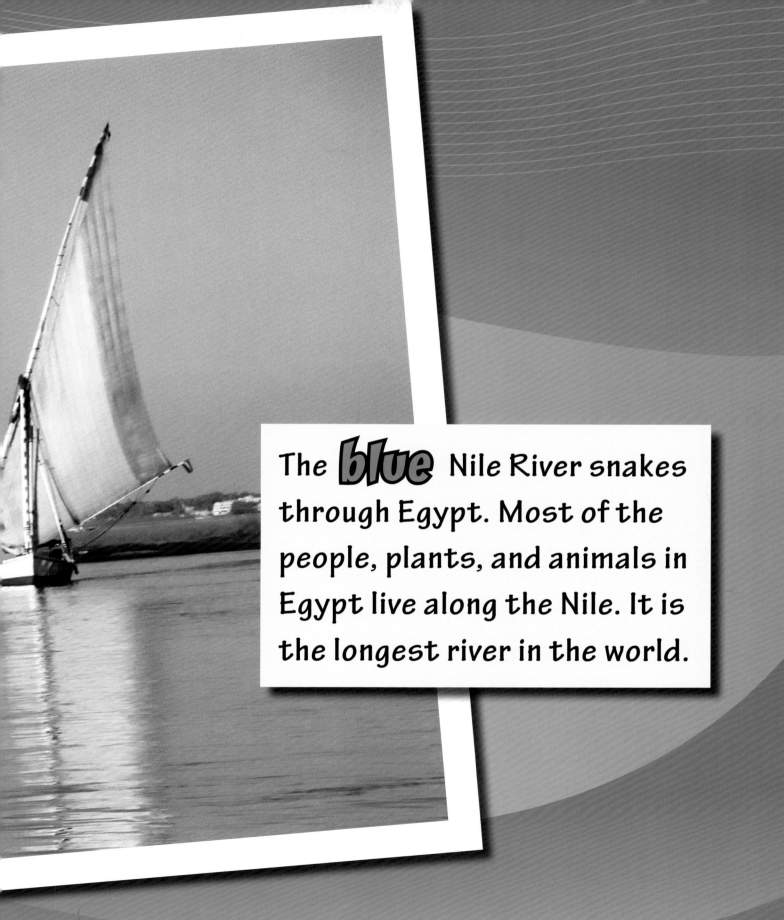

The **blue** Nile River snakes through Egypt. Most of the people, plants, and animals in Egypt live along the Nile. It is the longest river in the world.

Fluffy **white** cotton plants grow well in Egypt's warm and sunny farm fields. Egyptian cotton is sold all over the world. It is softer and stronger than many other types of cotton.

Yellow apartments line the busy street of an Egyptian city. Most families live in small city apartments. Houses are more common in the country.

The **white** dome of a mosque shines in the Cairo skyline. Cairo is the capital of Egypt. More people live in Cairo than in New York City.

An Egyptian soccer player in a **red** uniform races for the ball. Soccer is Egypt's most popular sport. The streets of Cairo are almost empty on game nights. Many fans stay at home to watch the games on TV.

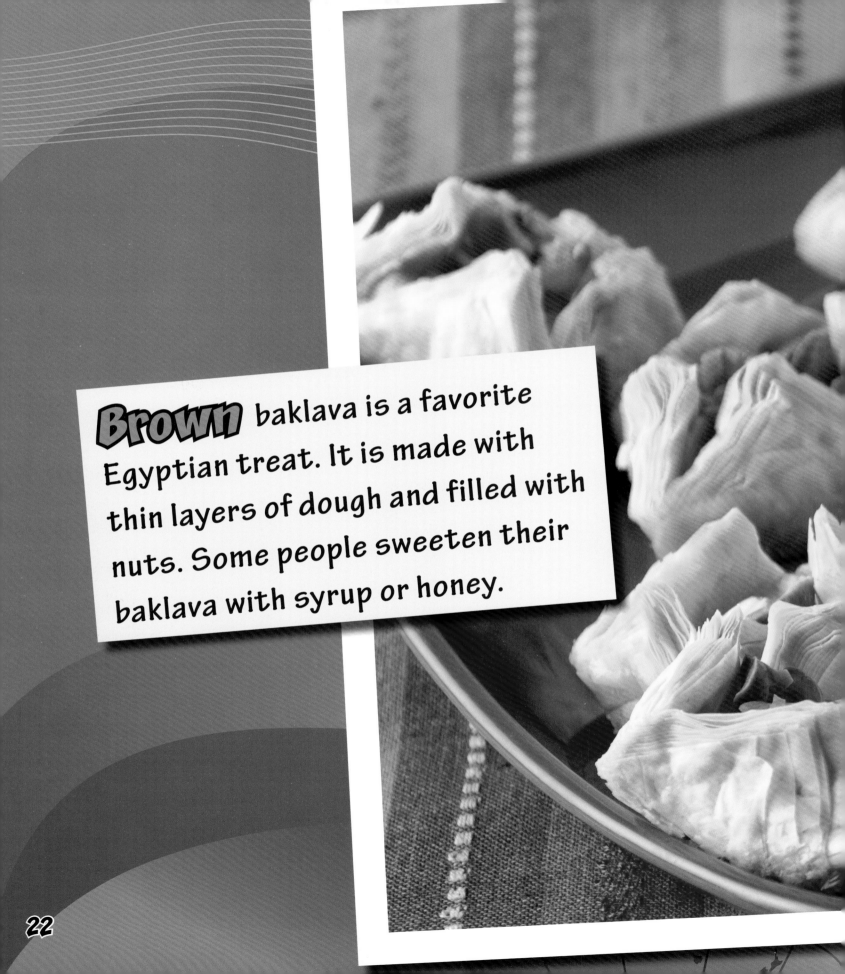

Brown baklava is a favorite Egyptian treat. It is made with thin layers of dough and filled with nuts. Some people sweeten their baklava with syrup or honey.

The **blue** water of the Suez Canal joins the Red Sea and the Mediterranean Sea. Ships use this shortcut to carry goods between Europe and Africa.

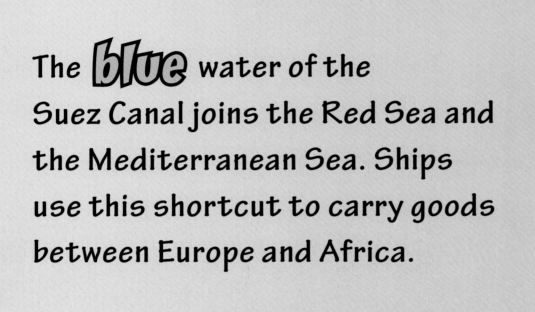

A dervish dancer in a **red** costume performs in an Egyptian market called a bazaar. Dervish dancers spin in circles while music plays. Some dancers also perform during Ramadan.

FACTS about Egypt

Capital City: Cairo

Population: 80,335,036

Official Language: Arabic

Common Phrases

English	Arabic	Pronunciation
please	min fadlak	(MIHN FAHD-lahk)
thank you	shukran	(SHUH-krahn)
yes	aywa	(EYE-wah)
no	laa	(LAH)

Map

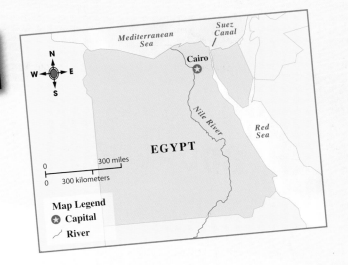

Flag

Money

Egyptian money is called the Egyptian pound. One pound equals 100 piastres.

Glossary

ancient (AYN-shunt) — from a long time ago

baklava (BOCK-lah-vah) — a sweet treat made of dough and filled with nuts

bazaar (buh-ZAR) — a street market

canal (kuh-NAL) — a channel that is dug across land; canals join bodies of water so that ships can travel between them.

dervish dancer (DUHR-vish DANSS-er) — a dancer who spins in circles while music plays; some perform during Ramadan.

dome (DOHM) — a round roof

fast (FAST) — to give up eating for a period of time

mosque (MOSK) — a building used by Muslims for worship

Muslim (MUHZ-luhm) — someone who follows the religion of Islam

pyramid (PIHR-uh-mid) — an ancient stone building where pharaohs and their treasures were buried

Ramadan (RAHM-i-dahn) — the holy month of the Islamic calendar; Muslims fast from sunrise to sunset during Ramadan.

Read More

Krebs, Laurie. *We're Sailing Down the Nile: A Journey through Egypt.* Cambridge, Mass.: Barefoot Books, 2007.

Ryan, Patrick. *Welcome to Egypt.* Welcome to the World. Mankato, Minn.: Child's World, 2008.

Internet Sites

FactHound offers a safe, fun way to find Internet sites related to this book. All of the sites on FactHound have been researched by our staff.

Here's how:

1. Visit *www.facthound.com*

2. Choose your grade level.

3. Type in this book ID **1429616997** for age-appropriate sites. You may also browse subjects by clicking on letters, or by clicking on pictures and words.

4. Click on the **Fetch It** button.

FactHound will fetch the best sites for you!

Index

32

A+ Books are published by Capstone Press,
151 Good Counsel Drive, P.O. Box 669, Mankato, Minnesota 56002.
www.capstonepress.com

1 2 3 4 5 6 13 12 11 10 09 08

Library of Congress Cataloging-in-Publication Data
Olson, Nathan.
  Egypt in colors / by Nathan Olson.
    p. cm. — (A+ books. World of colors)
    Summary: "Simple text and striking photographs present Egypt, its culture,
and its geography" — Provided by publisher.
    Includes bibliographical references and index.
    ISBN-13: 978-1-4296-1699-7 (hardcover)
    ISBN-10: 1-4296-1699-7 (hardcover)
    1. Egypt — Juvenile literature. 2. Egypt — Pictorial works — Juvenile literature. I. Title.
DT49.O47 2009
962 — dc22   2008005270

Credits
Megan Peterson, editor; Veronica Bianchini, designer; Wanda Winch, photo researcher

Photo Credits
Art Life Images/age fotostock/Doug Scott, 24–25; Art Life Images/age fotostock/J.D.
Dallet, 4–5, 12–13; Art Life Images/age fotostock/Sylvain Grandadam, 8–9; Capstone
Press/Karon Dubke, 22–23; fotolia/Mikhail Nekrasov, 18–19; Getty Images Inc./
AFP/Cris Bouroncle, 6–7; Getty Images Inc./AFP/Issouf Sanogo, 21; Getty Images
Inc./Lonely Planet Images/John Elk III, 16–17; iStockphoto/Karim Hesham, 2–3;
Paul Baker, 29 (coin); Peter Arnold Inc./SPOT, 10–11; Shutterstock/Laurin Rinder,
14–15; Shutterstock/Noel Powell, Schaumburg, cover (camel); Shutterstock/Petrof
Stanislav Eduardovich, 29 (banknote); Shutterstock/Pichugin Dmitry, cover (pyramid);
Shutterstock/Vera Bogaerts, 26–27; Shutterstock/Vladimir Korostyshevskiy, 1;
StockHaus Ltd., 29 (flag)

Note to Parents, Teachers, and Librarians
This World of Colors book uses full-color photographs and a nonfiction format
to introduce children to basic topics in the study of countries. *Egypt in Colors*
is designed to be read aloud to a pre-reader or to be read independently by an
early reader. Photographs help listeners and early readers understand the text
and concepts discussed. The book encourages further learning by including
the following sections: Facts about Egypt, Glossary, Read More, Internet Sites,
and Index. Early readers may need assistance using these features.